7 Principles for Raising Black Sons

A Practical Guide for Single Black Mothers

K. ESTELLE

ISBN-13: 978-0615903316
ISBN-10: 0615903312

DEDICATION

This book is dedicated to Trayvon Martin's family and to all the mothers who lost their sons to gang violence and police brutality. May God give you comfort knowing that your sons' souls are in a better place.

I also dedicate this book to the strongest person I have ever known, Mrs. M. Johnson. There are no words that can express my gratitude for all that you have done for me.

Thank you for giving me life.

CONTENTS

ACKNOWLEDGMENTS

First and foremost, I would like to give thanks to the Almighty for giving the ability to turn words into the reality of a dream. Second, my deepest appreciation and gratitude go out to my mother, M. Johnson, and to my father, L. Estelle, who worked diligently to raise me into the strong individual I am today. I thank my grandmother, Mrs. Sylvia Johnson, for being the rock of our family and for being there for me in my darkest moments. My love for you is greater than you'll ever know. Grandma Latisha Magee, I love you dearly. Aunt Deana, Aunt Joyce, and all the rest of my aunts and uncles, thank you for your support over the years. Jeremy Kennedy, R.I.P.

I would like to give a special shout out to my big cousin, Shelly Martin. You had my back when it mattered the most. I'll never forget all the love and support you gave in times of need. Dyihea Nicholson, thank you for being the ride or die chick you have been since day one. D'andre Allan, a.k.a. *Ghetto*, big bro', your loyalty will never go unappreciated. Brione' Rhodes, a.k.a. *Goodlyfe*, you are the truest brother I have ever encountered in all of my years. Your spiritual strength and power of mind should be something every black man in this country aspires to obtain. Eternal blessings to you and your family. Mary, you believed in me when no one else did. Thank you. Lil' Sis Ashlei, be strong, girl, and keep striving – forever love. Unc Tim, your heart is pure as gold, man – 1-luv.

Finally, I would like to thank Ms. Tierica 'Defyne' Berry for lending a helping hand with the completion of this project. You are a powerful sista' and I am deeply honored to have been able to work with you. If you ever need me, know, without a doubt, I got your back. Ms. Barard, my editor from Urban Book Editor LLC, you are an editor of the highest caliber. Thank you 100 times over (smile). Dada C. and Braylon, thank you for blessing the cover. The two of you truly exemplify what this book represents. Dada Raina u r powerful. POWER TO THE PEOPLE!

Papa Johnson, happy 80th, Big Guy! This one's for you!

INTRODUCTION – A MESSAGE TO THE NUBIAN MOTHERS

Across the United States, hundreds of thousands of adolescent, black males are being raised in households with young, black mothers struggling by themselves to rear their sons to be productive men of integrity and honor. These determined sisters are battling alone to provide for, protect, and teach their sons tactics to survive in a nation lacking compassion for the reality of their existence.

The single black mothers I am speaking of can be compared to that of a lonesome lioness in the jungle forced to hunt, feed, defend, nurture, and love her cubs without the support of a male counterpart. For these miraculously strong women, the constant struggle to steer their sons in the right direction and, at the same time, to shield them away from the pitfalls of the penal system, gang violence, suicidal fictions, and, even worse, death is a full time job. The single mother must also work a nine to five in order to pay bills and keep food on the table.

I wrote this book in an effort to provoke thought within the minds of these courageous sisters and to begin a discussion about creating new ways to teach single mothers how to raise their sons to become noble, strong, black men that they would be proud of.

My perspectives on what it takes for single, black women to raise their sons are, at times, hard-nosed. I write with a take no prisoners style that may offend some people. However, if you seek truth and understanding, then I am hopeful that by the time you have finished reading this book you will have gained something useful that you can meditate on and share with someone else.

Thank you.

PRINCIPLE 1 – JUST BECAUSE HIS FATHER WAS A DEADBEAT, DON'T BLAME YOUR SON

I'm sure you've heard the stories from black men who hold resentment toward their mothers for the emotional abuse they were forced to endure as young men. It seems as if every black man in America growing up in a single mother home has heard the echo of these phrases a time or two in their lifetime.

"Boy, get out my face! You look just like yo' damn daddy and I can't stand that no good ass man!"

"Boy, you just like your father. He wasn't shit and your bad ass ain't going to be shit either!"

These are just a couple of the types of phrases that some angry, single mother is probably shouting at their son even as you read this. Somewhere in the country at this moment there is a mother who has just been abandoned by the father of her child. She is angry, confused, depressed, and frustrated with the reality of having to fend for herself and rear a child on her own. Her feelings are justified. I can offer no excuse for a deadbeat father who is unwilling to take on the responsibility of a life that he took part in creating.

Single mothers have every right to feel rage, resentment, and frustration towards the men who have abandoned their children and them. However, these women must be careful not to transfer their anger and resentment onto their sons. The children are not at fault.

Genetics are utterly extraordinary. Some children come out of the womb looking like a mirror image of their parents. However, this can be a bad combination for young men growing up in single mother households if their mother constantly targets them as verbal punching bags to express their anger and resentment for being forced to parent alone.

Single mothers who subconsciously practice this form of self-therapy must understand that even though it makes them feel good to beat into their sons' minds how much of a loser their fathers are, they are only causing their son to hoard resentment and hatred towards them that can very well last a lifetime. Young males who are growing up fatherless already carry the burden of not feeling truly loved, important, and confident. They realize early on that something is wrong in their household, when they go to their friends' houses only to discover that Tommy's mother and father are together while his aren't. These young brothers receive a clear message that something is not right in their lives when on Father's Day all of their friends around the neighborhood are out celebrating with their dads while they sit at home with their mothers. Women raising their sons by themselves must realize that their sons don't need them to constantly inform them about how much of a deadbeat their biological fathers are.

As the years roll by and these young men grow older,

it becomes clear to them that their fathers were cowards. In a lot of cases, these young brothers grow to despise their fathers without any help from their mothers. Single moms must learn that just because their sons are mirror-images of the men who have hurt them deeply does not mean he has to be a reflection of the pain she feels. A son may have some of the qualities his father possessed. Yet, he is not destined to be just like his father.

Keep the anger you feel towards the father of your child between you, his father, and God. Leave your children out of it. I guarantee you that as your sons grow into manhood they will respect you for not bashing their father in front of them.

Women of integrity do not complain or emotionally abuse their children for the trials and tribulations that they experience in life. They stay strong and push forward using their children as instruments of inspiration. There is no harm in being honest parents. Informing them about the real reason of why there is no father figure in the home is acceptable, but be mindful not to over-explain. Young boys admire and respect mothers who tell them the truth about why their fathers are not in their lives, but they crumble into a life of depression and self-destruction when faced with mothers who chastise and persecute them for wrongful deeds their fathers committed. Single mothers struggling with this issue should seek counseling.

Sometimes when we suppress our pain, we turn into ticking time bombs waiting to explode. I've come to learn that a good old-fashioned conversation, a long cry, and a comforting shoulder to lean on can, at times, give you the power to let go and let God.

Here are a few mental exercises that can further help you jump the hurdle of dealing with this issue:

1.) When you look at your son and see the resemblance to his father take deep long breaths and pray. Ask God or Allah to bless you with the power of forgiveness. Just try it. You'll be surprised how fast God works sometimes.

2.) When you notice characteristics in your son that resemble his father, don't persecute him. Instead, bring it to his attention calmly. Be honest, but speak extremely carefully and sympathetically when explaining why that trait disturbs you. As your son gradually makes improvement in the areas you pointed out, praise him and if appropriate, reward him.

Remember: When you forgive those that have wronged or hurt you, God blesses you abundantly for your righteousness.

PRINCIPLE 2 –YOUR SON IS A BABY IN YOUR EYES, BUT DON'T TREAT HIM LIKE ONE

Everyone knows at least one man in their family who refuses to grow up and take responsibility for his own life. In some cases, these men are just lazy. They're doing their best to convince other people to give them a handout every chance they get. On the other hand, some of these men are the products of mothers who wouldn't allow them to properly mature and grow into manhood.

A good example of this is shown in the movie *Baby Boy*, directed by John Singleton and starring Tyrese and Taraji P. Henson. The film depicts the life of a man in his early twenties who has fathered two children by two different women. Tyrese's character, Jody, lives at home with his mother and only partially takes on his responsibilities as a father and, most importantly, a grown man. Jody, for the most part, is perfectly content with the free ride he is getting from his mother. His mother supports his immaturity rarely requiring her son to own up to his responsibilities and leave her home. Only when

Jody's mother finds a new boyfriend and problems begin to ensue between her son and her new companion that she finally forces Jody to leave. Searching deeper beneath the surface of this story it is probable that if Jody's mother had not found a "new" man in her life, she may not have been so eager to get him out of her home.

While writing this book I've researched and witnessed cases of grown black men between the ages of 30-35 still living with their mothers. They generally pay no rent, do not help with any bills or house chores, and in some cases are pampered and waited on as if they were still five-year-olds. Mothers, in general, and single moms, in particular, place their sons at a great disadvantage when they baby them. It prevents them from maturing into men.

Now, let's get deeper…

From the moment of their birth, Afrikan men in the United States are at a greater disadvantage than every group of people in the country. Black males, if they are to be successful in America, are forced to mature faster, to be extremely careful about how they handle situations they are placed in, and to work ten times harder than their competition. For black men in America there are no free rides or handouts. Therefore, mothers should ensure that their sons understand this reality. Starting at the age of at least six, single moms need to be stern and consciously dedicated to the concept of pushing their boys to become secure in their independence, confident in their problem-solving abilities, and aware of the fact that they deserve *only* what they earn in life.

Every time a young boy goes out to play and comes back home with a bruise or a cut on his knee, he does not need his mother to treat him like a baby. Being overly protective weakens the young man. Overprotectiveness undermines a man's ability to stoically withstand pain.

Single mothers should prepare first-aid kits and teach their sons how to bandage their own cuts and scrapes. When they get older and more serious injuries occur, they will be able to handle it and will not need Momma to baby them back to wellness. Please do not misinterpret what I am saying about this. It is perfectly normal for mothers to perceive their children as their babies for the rest of their lives, but mothers who treat their male children like babies even as they grow older may give their sons a handicap that can be challenging to overcome.

Single moms, please stop referring to your son as your baby. If your son is past the age of five, he is not a baby anymore. He is a young man who is growing, day by day, into a fully grown man. As human beings, we believe what we are called. If a mother calls her son *baby* all his life, he will expect her to treat him as such even into his adulthood. Boys, especially Afrikan boys, must be groomed into manhood. In most cases, grown men who are perceived as *momma's boys* became that way because their mothers were over-protective. I'm sure you've all heard of men who were referred to as *soft*, *weak-hearted*, or *a girl with boxers on*. These are all definitions and labels for men who have not properly evolved into manhood. Boys who are over-protected by their mothers often are teased by their peers and may suffer socially.

I have seen countless examples of these types of men. Men who don't know how to interact with other men, throw temper tantrums when they don't get their way, are scared to defend themselves, and run home to their mothers every time they face a problem are classic examples of men who were raised by a mother who subconsciously robbed them of their maturity and toughness as a man. Certainly, not all men who have these characteristics fit into this category; however, a good percentage do.

In closing, I ask all of you single mothers to pay closer attention to your interactions with your sons. Push them to be independent, tough, confident in their own abilities, and to understand that everyone in your household pays their own way in one way or another. When you refuse to allow your son to grow up, you dig him into a hole that can be hard for him to escape. If your grown son is not in school, is unemployed, and is still living with you, make him do chores around the house to earn his keep. If your son is working, make him pay the cable bill, water bill, or somehow contribute to the household financially. This will teach him that there are no free rides in this world. Women who understand this fact and are diligent in ensuring that their boys comprehend this will have sons who grow up to be successful in life.

A lot of experts claim that single, black mothers are incapable of raising their sons into strong, productive men. Don't believe that. Many women who were in the same position you are in now chose to be stern, hard, and relentless with their boys. They were tough but that helped transform their young boys into extraordinary men. Adolescent Afrikan males must be fearless if they want to survive. It is unfair to single moms who must carry the burden of teaching their sons these things themselves; however, it is a reality that they must tackle if they desire for their sons to succeed.

Here are a few mental exercises that can further help you with the topic of this chapter:

1.) Never allow your son to break his word about something he said he would do. Teach your son that a real man is nothing without the honor of his word. Men must be taught this trait at an early age if they are to retain it into adulthood. Start teaching this lesson now!

2.) Keep first aid kits in a designated area of the house. Teach him only a couple times how to clean and bandage the minor injuries he receives while playing outside in the neighborhood. Make him care for himself. Toughness is essential to young men entering their manhood. Don't let your son's toughness slip away.

3.) Teach your son how to cook. This can be a fun way to introduce him on how to become more independent. From time to time, make him prepare a basic meal for you. Praise his efforts. It will be a good experience for the both of you. Besides, if he gets good at it, you won't have to cook so often!

PRINCIPLE 3 – LEAVE ROOM FOR DIALOGUE

In many urban communities in the U.S. there are alarming levels of violent crime. Every day of their lives, adolescent Afrikan males are faced with the possibility of their lives ending prematurely. Whether it's a tragedy like the police brutality exerted against Sean Bell or Trayvon Martin being murdered while walking home from the store, levels of violence against young Afrikan men is at crisis levels. Black males also have to contend with the possibility of imprisonment either due to trumped-up charges or over-zealous prosecution by judicial systems determined to destroy black communities. Black men of all ages face endless possibilities for their lives to be flipped upside down by injustice and violence. All black mothers face this issue along with their sons. Single mothers feel this burden more acutely because they are solely accountable for their sons 100 percent of the time.

Seventeen-year-old Trayvon Martin was profiled by 28-year-old Mark Zimmerman. An overly-aggressive neighborhood watch member, Zimmerman stalked Martin and instigated a fight with the young man, even after being told to stand down by a 911 dispatcher whom he had called for advice. Subsequently, a jury found that Zimmerman shot and killed teenage Trayvon Martin justifiably. Zimmerman's defense attorneys described Martin as a malicious thug who attacked Zimmerman for *no apparent reason.* Zimmerman's attorneys used a common stereotype, the *dangerous black man*, which the U.S. judicial system has used successfully for over 500 years, and counting, to murder and imprison Afrikan men at record numbers.

The truth of the matter is that Trayvon Martin was a good kid who came from a good family. Both his mother and father were active in his life. His promising future was cut short by an ignorant, trigger-happy individual who mistakenly profiled him as a criminal. Surveillance videos before the murder shows Trayvon Martin purchasing a can of ice tea and a small bag of Skittles candy. The sad part about the whole thing is that teenage Martin probably did not imagine as he left the convenience store that, in a matter of minutes, he would lose his life so viciously. It is an undeniable fact that no other group of people in American society faces the number of these types of tragedies that black men face.

So, what does this mean for single, Afrikan women who are raising sons on their own?

First, it means that your son, if he is not careful about the way he positions himself in society, could suffer the same senseless fate as Trayvon Martin. It's been proven time and time again by the murder of Malcolm X, Martin Luther King Jr., Tupac Shakur, and millions of other Afrikan brothers who were hung from trees as a form of entertainment, that a black man's life in American society means nothing. If we, as a black community, do not begin to stress the importance of our survival, who will?

There is a dire need for single mothers to leave room for dialogue with their sons. All mothers are aware of how stubborn and hard-headed teenage boys can be when they start to perceive themselves as men. Starting around the age of thirteen, many boys begin to feel as though they don't have to answer to anyone. They push their parents, especially single mothers, in a bid for independence. A lot of times they get into troublesome situations as they rush into a world that they are not completely ready for.

Throughout the process of writing this book, I interviewed a number of black males between the ages of thirteen to eighteen who were being reared by single mothers. Over 75 percent of these young men regularly got into trouble with their moms for not following household rules and for doing things their own way, even if it meant going against their mothers wishes. I asked these young men to explain to me a few of the reasons why they are disobedient and what they would like their mothers to do better in their eyes.

The majority of the boys said that their mothers were too strict and that they tried to keep them in the house too much. They also expressed that they felt it was hard to tell their moms anything; they were afraid their mothers would hold it against them. Although I informed them that there is no explanation under the sun for disrespecting and undermining the direction of their mothers, I think it is essential to examine the thought patterns of these young men.

Black males growing up without a father at home lack the understanding of fear and discipline from a superior male, unless it is enforced elsewhere. This explains why single mothers feel the need to put their foot down in an alpha-male way. They do this to ensure they get respect from their sons. This is an element within the single mother- son dynamic that, for the most part, I absolutely agree with. Every mother, single or not, needs to establish some method to maintain the appropriate level of respect and order in their households. Without this, the child(ren) will become a threat to himself and to her. Without discipline, a young man will eventually self-destruct, because he does not understand the rules and guidelines that we must abide by in order to live freely in society. If single moms do not instill discipline in their sons before they leave home, the local law enforcement authorities won't mind teaching the young men the lessons they weren't properly taught at home.

On the flip side of this issue, single mothers must also be conscious of not being too strict with their boys. They must find appropriate ways to leave room for conversation. Applying pressure is necessary for a young man's development, but too much pressure can, over time, have a negative effect. When a mother is too strict and overly-aggressive with her son, it makes the young man envision his mother as the enemy. Therefore, he will rebel at every opportunity. Moms should dispense punishments only when absolutely necessary, not for every minor offense.

This strategy explains the principle of leaving room for dialogue. It has been proven that adolescent black males who grow up in environments where they can express their views and opinions without the fear of being ridiculed by their parents are less likely to experience jail or develop a criminal record. On the contrary, boys who grow up in stressful settings where they are forced to suppress their thoughts and opinions, suffer a higher probability of having run-ins with the law.

When it comes to uncomfortable topics, such as sex,

violence, race, and other controversial subjects, don't be afraid to have discussions about it. It is extremely important to establish a healthy line of communication with your son. A situation might arise in the future where your son feels comfortable enough to confide in you about the potential of something bad happening, giving you the ability to stop it before it happens. Mothers who establish this type of communication early on in their child's life benefit the most from these situations.

The communication level between single, black mothers and their sons is an area of that requires serious improvement. Open communication can decrease the suicide, homicide, and rape accusations faced by black men. As a kid, I had a great line of communication with my mother. She can testify that if you leave room for dialogue, your son will reach out when it matters most. Whether I was facing a good situation or a bad one, I knew I could depend on my mother to listen. I can't begin to tell you how many times she talked me out of doing stupid things as a teenager.

Scientifically, it has been proven that women hold greater intellectual capabilities than men. Use those great minds you have, ladies. Get inside your sons' minds and figure out what's going on in there. If something is disturbing him, you should be the first to know. It's true that women can't teach boys everything about becoming a man, but don't let that stop you from being a voice of reason in your son's life. He desperately needs your insight. If he doesn't have it, he will be forced to learn everything on his own or in the mean streets.

(Single moms) + (Their Sons) + (Communication) =

{A greater chance those moms can prevent something bad from happening}

Try these three exercises to help improve communication with your son:

1.) At least two days each week, make your son sit down and have a healthy conversation with you. Even if things seem uneasy at first, keep working at it. Practice makes perfect. Over time, your son will begin to get comfortable speaking with you.

2.) Find ways to laugh and joke with your son as much as possible. Allow him to feel as though you are someone he can relate to. This is a balancing act. At the same time, you must make sure his respect level for you remains intact.

3.) If you can't get through to your son with dialogue, find someone who can. Try going to an uncle, an aunt, a cousin, or enroll him in a big brother program. Work at finding someone who can get through to him and relay important information to you, so you can better understand what is going on inside your son's head.

PRINCIPLE 4 –YOUR SON IS NOT YOUR BOYFRIEND

There is a new type of Afrikan man. These men do not respect their mothers. When I was a kid, all of the men in my family displayed the utmost respect for their mothers. I was taught by the men in my family that if I ever wanted "a for sure ass-whooping" all I had to do was let them find out I had disrespected my mother. As far back as I can remember, it was instilled in me that no matter what my mother said or did, even if I did not agree with it, I was never to over step my boundaries as her son by displaying any form of disrespect.

There are many reasons why so many young black men growing up in single mother households do not maintain a high level of respect for their mothers. One particular issue I would like to point out is that many black women treat their teenage boys like their boyfriend rather than their son.

Here are a few examples of this behavior:

- Mothers who curse their teenage sons out when they get upset with them; they are treating their sons like low-down boyfriends they can't stand.

- Single moms who smoke marijuana with their teenaged sons.
- Mothers who lavish expensive gifts on their boys in an attempt to buy their love.

All of these are classic examples of single moms confusing their sons with a lover or a companion. I point these issues out not to ridicule, but to shed light on the bigger issue that needs to be addressed – the lack of respect young brothers of this new generation have toward their mothers.

Half the blame for this situation lies with the mothers who are raising these young men. Too many women allow their sons to back talk them starting at young ages. Too many single moms spoil their sons with gifts as a substitute for love and affection or because they think that giving their son whatever they desire will make them behave better. When these young men reach adulthood, they often are no good to themselves or to the women whose lives they enter.

I advise all the single mothers who are reading this book to do whatever is necessary and within reasonable limits to get a handle of your sons' behavior at the earliest age possible. Even if your son is a toddler, don't allow him to do whatever he pleases. He should not be allowed to talk back to you when you give him instruction. In the long run, if you allow the negative behavior the situation will only get worse. Your son will begin to adopt the mentality that you are a companion rather than his mother. That, then, enables him to think that if he is not in agreement with an instruction you've given, then he has justification to ignore it. Any mother who does not maintain order and authority in her home does not have a son at all. On the contrary, she simply has a young man living for free inside her home who thinks that she is his woman and he can do whatever he wants when he chooses to. This is not an opinion or an assumption, but a fact. Anyone who doesn't believe me can do some research. Ask the single moms who have absolutely no control of their boys and are stressed out constantly as a result.

Next, let's address the single moms who curse their sons out like they are no good men in the street. The majority of women who do this are only trying to establish authority and control, but you must realize that this can have a negative effect on your son. A young man who day after day is belittled, made fun of, and verbally abused by his own mother can potentially become a man who displays no respect for women at all. He also can develop a disdain for his mother that may never perish. Young brothers who are physically and verbally abused by their mothers may also explain why the percentages for domestic violence and rape are so high.

Boys, especially teenage boys, can be hard-headed thorns in the side. I understand. I am in no way implying that moms shouldn't give their sons a good tongue lashing every now and again but, ladies, please be careful about the words you use and how harshly you lash out. Gauge your level of anger. Learn how to identify when you may lose control and learn to stop yourself before it happens. Not only will this give you a healthy balance of self-control but it will teach your son self-control as well.

As part of the research that was done while writing this book, I spoke with some young brothers who were still in high school (some of them were as young as ninth graders) who confided that their single mothers smoke marijuana with them on a regular basis and even allowed them to engage in casual sex with their teenage girlfriends in the home. Mothers who practice this type of behavior do not know the danger they could possibly be creating for their boys and themselves.

Marijuana is not a recreational drug anymore. It may have been in the 70s, 80s, and early 90s. Today, kids are physically and mentally addicted to this drug. Mothers who smoke weed with their sons, especially before their boys' brains have fully developed, increase the potential of drug addiction when their sons are older. Over 50% of teenagers who start out smoking marijuana before the age of eighteen continue to smoke far into their late twenties and early thirties.[1]

Frequently, I hear parents raising teenagers say, "I would rather my child smoke weed and do drugs with me in the comfort of my own home rather than they do it out in the streets where they can potentially get in trouble." Parents who think this way are not thinking logically. Allowing their teenage sons to do drugs in the home with them does not prevent them from doing drugs out in the streets with their friends. If your child feels comfortable rolling blunts in front of you at home, he will feel comfortable doing it outside the home as well. Ladies, give your son the opportunity to make the mistakes or experiment with drugs on their own. Please don't promote it in the home. In the long run, you will only be robbing your son of a fully-developed and well-functioning mind.

Lastly, I would like to address the single mothers who allow their sons to have casual sex inside their own home. Again, ladies, I understand what you are thinking. Some

---

1 "Who are you? U.S. Government Statistics on Adult Marijuana Users", By Russ Belville, accessed April 15, 2009, http://www.cannabisculture.com/content/who-are-you-us-government-statistics-marijuana-users.html

of you may believe that you are only trying to help the situation by creating a better environment for your sons to experiment with sex. But, what happens when these young girls become pregnant? What happens when your immature and incompetent teenage son has a baby but doesn't have the slightest clue about how to become a healthy father because he, himself, has never had one?

Mothers who promote their boys having sex inside their own homes are headed for disaster. Millions of adults today were born to teenage parents who were too immature and financially unstable to properly raise them. These children grew up to live hard and stressful lives. Some of them made it out of the hell of a life they were born into, but a lot of them didn't.

All of these issues are realities we have no choice but to face and tackle head on or else the number of teenage pregnancies will only continue to get higher. Single moms must identify early on in their son's development that he is not her companion or imaginary mate but her son, and only her son. Single mothers must prevent their sons from thinking that they too have a voice of authority when it comes to listening to her instruction. This only breeds dysfunction in the single-parent household and develops grown men who have little or no respect for the voice of the mothers that gave them life.

Try these exercises to further help you, if needed:

1.) Completely eliminate back talking. Punish him by taking away privileges that you know will affect your son when he tries to undermine your authority. You must make him realize that the household you run is not a democracy, but a dictatorship that you oversee.

2.) Be careful not to divulge too much information about your personal life to your son. If too much is revealed, he can potentially lose respect for you.

3.) Don't shower your son with lavish gifts. Allow him to earn those things. A boy who grows up being spoiled by his mother thinks that every woman he deals with should do the same and acts like a spoiled brat when he doesn't get his way. Make your son work for nice things. Don't give them to him so easily.

PRINCIPLE 5 – TOUGH LOVE BUILDS STRONG BLACK MEN

Expecting excellence from your son should be the norm. There's nothing wrong with making your son do things over and over again until he masters the task at hand. Whether it's making your sons clean their rooms, wash dishes, do school work, or practice a specific sport, don't be afraid to push your sons to their limits. They need this and, when they are adults, will appreciate you for doing so. All the lessons you teach them early on about chasing perfection, not settling for mediocrity, and doing things the right way the first time around will benefit them when they enter the real world.

When I was in middle school, I confided in my mother that I was going to try out for the school basketball team. I had a full week to prepare for try-outs, but I didn't practice very much at first. When my mother saw this, she tore into my behind for being lazy. For the rest of the week, she drove me to a nearby park and made me play pick-up games with grown men at the park from sun up until sun down. I was so frustrated with my mother for pushing me so hard. I was getting beat up on the court pretty bad by the older guys, but I learned some great lessons about getting rebounds and handling the basketball better. Needless to say, when tryouts came around, I made the team effortlessly. It was all thanks to my mother who wouldn't allow me to be lazy. She was relentless in making sure I understood that success in anything didn't come without sweat and hard work. My gratitude towards her for teaching me this is immeasurable. These lessons benefited me tremendously as I matured because I already had developed the confidence of knowing that if I worked hard enough I could accomplish anything.

We need more of these types of life lessons for our next generation of sons, who will lead the way in the black man's progressive movement. Some women are afraid of holding their sons accountable for chasing excellence. They view it as being too hard on their sons or being too strict. I suggest you think of it this way: Your son doesn't have a father figure in his life. So, if you don't do it, who will?

A great percentage of black men today suffer from the disease of pure laziness. They weren't taught at an early age that legitimate hard work was indeed a way out of the gutter. This explains why so many seek selling drugs, robbing stores, and extorting their own communities as reasonable career choices. Changing this low level thinking among adolescent black males begins with making them understand that seeking perfection should be a daily practice. I'm not saying to teach them that they must be perfect. Instead, I suggest teaching them to do tasks to the best of their ability and to not stop practicing until they are satisfied with the quality of their work.

Mental toughness is an essential personality characteristic that all black boys need in order to become strong black men. Powerful Afrikan men like Martin Luther King Jr., Malcolm X, Fred Hampton, and Barack Obama were able to succeed against all odds because of their ability to remain mentally strong despite all the trials and tribulations that plagued them along their journeys to reaching the top of the mountain.

Be diligent in pushing your boys to the brink of exhaustion every chance you can. Life in America for black men is not a 100 meter race, but a marathon of great endurance, long suffering, and sheer will to cross the finish line. Single moms need to be the driving force behind the future of the young black brothers who will transcend the game into higher levels of success that we have never witnessed before.

It all starts with the minor things at home like chores, school work, maintaining one's word at all times, and never allowing your son to be lazy when he can be doing something productive. When your son trips over his feet and falls in your presence don't be so quick to give him a helping hand getting up. Instead, make him pick himself up off the ground. Again, this is an exercise in mental toughness. When your son grows up and he falls at certain times in life, he won't need anyone to help him get back up. He will already be equipped to do so himself. What you teach your sons early in childhood will be retained and used later in life.

It is not easy or fair for single mothers to carry the burden of raising a boy into manhood alone. Despite the challenges, there are a number of single women who are raising their sons on their own with great success. Some of the strongest people of will and spirit whom I have met in this world were women. Your ability to bleed every month, push through nine months of pregnancy, and still possess the determination to protect your children even if it means death, gives you a level of toughness that most men could never measure up to. All of you possess the ability to pass this mental strength on to your children. Point your sons in the right direction and Mother Nature will take care of the rest.

Try these mental exercises to help you teach your son how to develop his own mental strength and grow into an unstoppable force:

1.) Make your son set completion dates for new goals he wishes to achieve. Monitor his day to day progress and, if he slacks off, ride his coat tail relentlessly until he improves his focus on the task.

2.) Never allow your son to whine or complain to you about things he has the ability to change or control. Refuse to allow him to contract the disease of making excuses.

3.) Enroll your son in martial arts or boxing classes. Every young boy should learn how to defend himself. Combat sports teach toughness and discipline.

PRINCIPLE 6 – EVERY MAN YOU DATE DOES NOT NEED TO MEET YOUR SON

There's an old saying that goes, "Every person you date does not need to meet your mother!" Well, the same rule applies for single mothers with sons. Be very particular about the men you introduce to your son. It is extremely important that any man you bring into your household is going to be a positive male figure for the sustainable future. A lot of single mothers make the mistake of bringing home men who honestly have no intention of staying around for the long run. This sends a bad message to the boys who are growing up without a consistent father figure in their life. It teaches them that it's okay to be promiscuous and have numerous mates. No mother should want her son to think that.

Kids are accustomed to picking up habits, both good and bad, they see on a consistent basis. If a child grows up witnessing their parent frequently engaging with multiple sex partners, then they are more likely to practice the same thing. Whether you know it or not, your children watch your every move. Single moms have to be extra careful. Your sons may hold his feelings inside when he sees something that disturbs him. A boy who doesn't have a father figure to inform him that his mother is not his woman naturally thinks that she is. Although the son is wrong in his understanding of the relationship between his mother and himself, he does not know it. In many instances mothers are not trained to understand the emotions that are felt by her son, so therefore they go unacknowledged.

Whenever you bring a new man into your life, your son views him as an intruder – someone on the verge of taking his woman and the attention that is rightfully his. This upsets him, but over time he begins to get used to the new situation. He even might decide that he likes the new boyfriend. Things seem to be going well and your son finally is starting to get a taste of what it is like to have a fun-loving male figure in his life. Then, BOOM! It's over. The cool man he became accustomed to is gone. Mom has replaced him with a new intruder that the son has no choice but to deal with. As the years pass, the son matures and starts lose respect for his mother. The mother-son dynamic becomes strained and in some cases, irreparable.

Scenarios like this are plaguing thousands of adolescent males across the country daily. The real tragedy about the situation is that they don't properly understand the emotions they feel nor do they have anyone in their lives to accurately explain it to them. So, they hold everything inside and eventually determine that suppressing their feelings is the best way to handle their problems. Anger, frustration, confusion, and stress become everyday emotions for them which they carry into manhood.

Single moms, it is perfectly fine to take your time when dating someone new. Properly feel these men out before you invite them into your homes to meet your sons. Don't allow any man to rush you into moving too fast. Ten times out of ten, if a man has no regard about the well-being of you and your son, it's pretty certain that he is only after one thing. And, we all know what that is. A lot of times, if you just take the time to sit back and wait, these men will reveal their true intentions. If a man is only after sex, I assure you that if he doesn't get it as fast as he wants he won't stay around too long. If you meet a man who doesn't mind waiting and proving his worth until you are absolutely ready to bring him into your home, then nine times out of ten he is someone you can have a future with. Be careful in the beginning. Don't let your guard down. Some guys will put on a good guy persona and even play the patient game with you, but when they get what they want the real bad guy comes to the surface. Whether it takes two, three, or even six months to learn the true intentions of the new man you are dating, don't be afraid or ashamed to take your time. A real man with a sense of morality will applaud you for your conscientiousness and will be enticed to pursue you even more.

Still, you are a grown woman. Just because you are a single mother does not mean that you can't to do things grown people do. Just consider and respect your son in the process. You may be dating someone for simple fun that you are really not trying to get serious with. You may be having casual sex with a person you know in your heart you don't have a future with. If that's the case, it's okay. For some women these are realities, but it doesn't make them bad mothers. In this day and age, most Americans have experienced casual sex with someone they have no intention of marrying or starting a family with.

You are a single mother but you are still entitled to enjoy a personal life apart from your son. Do the things in life you enjoy doing but don't allow your son to know about it. Be discrete. Don't have casual sex in your home. Do those types of things far away from him or at least when he is not present in the household. In the eyes of a son, a mother is the purest entity they envision before reaching adulthood and having children of their own. Remember, your image and reputation to your son means everything to him. Don't do careless things around him to tarnish it.

Try these exercises to get a better view of the new men you want to bring into your home with your son:

1.) Give yourself at least 90 days to properly feel out the new guy you are dating. If after those 90 days you are still unsure about his intentions, extend the time until you feel sure of his true intentions.

2.) When the time comes that you do find a person you want to begin a new future with, have a long conversation with your son and carefully explain the situation. Give him the confidence he needs to adapt to the new situation.

3.) The first time you introduce your new man to your son, make it a date for all three of you. Go someplace like an amusement park where the attention is focused on your son rather than on the new man and you.

PRINCIPLE 7 –SEARCH FOR A BIG BROTHER PROGRAM OR A JEGNA TO HELP TEACH THE THINGS YOU CAN'T

There's no denying that there are just some things a woman cannot teach a boy about transitioning into manhood. Issues such as sex, sports, having negative run-ins with other boys, and attaining manhood can be difficult topics for single mothers to address with their sons on their own. Black men, especially men who were raised by single mothers, understand this. Big brother programs and other services tailored to adolescent black males are offered across the country.

I have chosen to use the Afrikan word *jegna* instead of the English word *mentor*. Originally, mentor was used in Ancient Greece to refer to an adult male instructor who offered his advice and tutelage in return for homosexual favors from his student. Jegna is a more appropriate word for Afrikans to use. Jegna means a courageous individual who is dedicated to the protection of his/her people, land, and culture. The term was used by such scholars as Mama Mirimba Ani and Dr. Asa Hilliard.

Over the years, programs like these have aided community non-violence drives and have helped black males go to college rather than become statistics in the penal system. Black men in major cities across the U.S. are sacrificing their time and are passionate about doing their best to reach at-risk youth to help them grow into productive citizens. We need many more such men but that fact does not take credit away from the legions of brothers standing strong on the front lines doing their part in the struggle. Single mothers should do the research in their home towns and find community groups for their sons. Community centers, churches, sports programs, and privately-run jegna programs are easy to find. Be diligent in your search. With time, I'm sure you will find someone sincere who can relate to your son on a level that he needs in his life.

Before selecting a jegna or big brother figure, have a lengthy conversation with these men and feel them out as you would any man who you intend on introducing to your son. Be mindful that there are some pedophiles and molesters out here in the world that we must keep a watchful eye out for. When selecting a jegna get first and last names and don't hesitate to do a background check if it makes you feel more comfortable. Although most big brother programs screen these men thoroughly, I advise you take the time to do a background check yourself if you feel the need to do so.

Try to find men who are college graduates. I say this because every mom should want her son to go continue their education after high school. Who better to steer him in the right direction than someone who has already done it themselves? At the same time, it is no big deal if you don't find that type of jegna. You can have expectations, but don't be too picky. Some of the best big brother jegnas I have met were ex-felons who turned their lives around to make positive contributions to their community and to ensure that young brothers don't make the same mistakes they did. The most important thing to look for is a man with a positive outlook on life who can relate to your son in a way that will drive him to listen and apply new lessons learned. If, by chance, you are not having much luck finding a jegna then search amongst your family and friends. Sometimes stepfathers, uncles, older cousins, and family friends can be the best role models for boys growing up in a single mother household.

Start out the relationship by allowing your son and his jegna to have one-on-one conversations in the comfort of your own home or at a recreational center until the jegna gains your trust. Gradually, you can allow them to set dates to do things on their own accord. If there are specific topics of conversation you would like your son's jegna to discuss during meetings then express them to the jegna. I'm sure he will be more than willing to do as you ask.

When I was 16 years old, I was struggling to find myself and traveling down a fast road to self-destruction and academic failure. I confess that if it had not been for my big brother, Minister Graves, who spent his spare time with me on a consistent basis, I would not be here today. Be open-minded. Big brother programs can work. And, they can take some of the heavy load off your shoulders. Give it a try.

EPILOGUE

Many people have concluded that a woman cannot raise a boy into a strong man. I am here to tell you that my own mother shattered that assumption into millions of pieces. Not only did my mother raise her young son to be a strong man but what is even more impressive is that she did it with all the chips stacked against her. And, she is not alone. Millions of single mothers across the country are doing the same thing. With a conscious mind, the right principles to teach, and a determined will any mother who exemplifies strength can transfer that mindset to her own son. Apply these seven principles to your everyday life and be relentless about teaching them to your sons. Remember that boys need discipline, a constant voice of authority, and a sense of mental toughness in order to battle through all the rain and pain black men must face in American society.

There is no time for excuses. There is no time for laziness. There is no time for grown men acting like spoiled and ungrateful brats. If black men of this next generation intend to survive, they must be strong, intelligent, and respect women. Single mothers, don't worry about the things you can't control but be purposeful about controlling the things you can. I know that it gets hard and sometimes you want to give up but always know in your heart that women are some of the strongest-willed creatures God ever created.

We, your sons, look at you in awe. Trust that as your sons grow older there will be no limit to their appreciation for the sacrifices you have made to ensure they survive the test of time.

No matter how hard things get, search for new ways to stay motivated. Don't hold feelings and emotions inside. Don't live trapped in despair. When you have things on your mind, find someone you can trust and confide in them, whether a therapist, brother, sister, friend, or church minister. Figure out a way to release those thoughts from your brain. Issues and problems held inside only cause confusion.

Pray for your children's father who abandoned you. Maintaining hatred towards these men only gives them power over you. Praying for them gives you God's grace and he will surely bless you.

Lastly, my Nubian Queens, teach your sons to aim high towards the sky and to never chase goals without a plan. My mother drilled into my head all the days of my life that "a man who failed to plan was a man who planned to fail!" Remember this wisdom and share it with your sons.

Blessings and good health to all of you.

ABOUT THE AUTHOR

K. Estelle is a novelist, poet, and curriculum writer. Originally from Michigan, Estelle now lives in Atlanta, Georgia. You can contact him with questions about this book or future projects at: NextLevelBooks@gmail.com.

Made in United States
Orlando, FL
30 March 2023

31526443R00026